Presented to

___

On the occasion of

___

From

___

Date

___

*To Tom, who showed me
how to put love on the menu*

ISBN 1-55748-779-0

All Scripture quotations are from the Authorized King James Version of the Bible unless otherwise noted.

Member of the
Evangelical Christian
Publishers Association

Published by Barbour and Company, Inc.
P.O. Box 719
Uhrichsville, Ohio 44683

Printed in the United States of America.

Comfort
FOOD

*Come home
to wholesome foods
that make you feel good*

Compiled and written by
Ellen W. Caughey

A Barbour Book

Contents

Introduction

Can you really go home again? That's a pretty tired question, but then again, many of us are just too stressed to ponder deep issues. Or even ones bobbing near the surface. Like, what's for dinner?

Can you really go home again? If home means the minute you open the door delightful aromas embrace you. If home means a kitchen brimming with naturally low-fat fresh ingredients, pots bubbling over, and a warm oven ready to welcome a casserole or pie. If home means living day to day, come what may, with Jesus Christ as your Savior.

You're there now. Back home. The original comfort zone. The kitchen of *Comfort Food*.

Lean on Me Lentil Soup

*...For the Lord seeth not as man seeth; for man looketh
on the outward appearance, but the Lord looketh
on the heart. (1 Samuel 16:7)*

1 cup lentils

4 cups chicken broth, fresh or canned

One bay leaf

2 TB unsalted butter

One large white onion

One 28-ounce can Italian tomatoes, plus liquid

Two medium potatoes, peeled and diced

Two hot dogs, uncooked

Place lentils and chicken broth in large saucepan with bay leaf and bring to a boil. Reduce heat and simmer covered for 1 1/2 hours. Check lentils occasionally to see if more broth is required and add if necessary. Remove bay leaf. Melt butter in small saute pan, and cook onion until soft. Add to lentils, along with tomatoes and their liquid and potatoes. Simmer soup for another 45 minutes. A few minutes before serving, add hot dogs and heat through.

Serves four to six, and (this goes without saying) is even more comforting when reheated.

Comfort Food

Winter Vegetable Soup

Then Job answered the Lord, and said, I know that thou canst do every thing, and that no thought can be withholden from thee. (Job 42:1, 2)

13 cups water

One large white onion, diced

Two beef soup bones with some meat on them

9 tsp instant beef bouillon

One 28-ounce can peeled Italian tomatoes, with juice

One 8-ounce can tomato sauce

4 cups cut green beans

1 1/2 cups peas

2 cups sliced carrots

1 cup diced yellow or green zucchini

1/2 cup chopped celery

Put water, onion, and soup bones in large pot and cook several hours until meat is pulling off bones. Let stand overnight in refrigerator so fat will harden on top. Remove hardened fat and discard. Pull meat off bones; discard bones. Cut meat into small pieces and return to liquid.

Add bouillon, tomatoes, and tomato sauce to liquid; mash or cut up tomatoes into bite-size pieces. Heat well. Add beans, peas, carrots, zucchini, and celery; cook until they are soft but not mushy. Taste and adjust seasoning by adding more of the above ingredients or salt and pepper.

Serve with Cheddar cheese and crackers or crusty french bread. Makes twelve generous servings.

Therese H. Cerbie

Chili con Hearty

*...Hast thou not heard, that the everlasting God, the Lord,
the Creator of the ends of the earth, fainteth not, neither is weary?...
He giveth power to the faint; and to them that have no might
he increaseth strength. (Isaiah 40:28, 29)*

1 pound lean ground beef

1 cup white onion, chopped

Two cloves garlic, minced

3 cups water

1 cup thinly sliced carrots

One green bell pepper, chopped

One 4-ounce can chopped green chilies, undrained

One 6-ounce can tomato paste

2 TB chili powder

1/2 tsp salt

Comfort Food

1 tsp oregano

1 tsp cumin

Black pepper to taste

One 28-ounce can Italian peeled tomatoes, torn roughly,
    with juice

One to two 16-ounce can(s) red kidney beans, rinsed
    and drained (depending on your taste)

In a large soup pot brown the meat with the onion and garlic over medium heat. Drain off excess fat and return meat mixture to pot. Add the remaining ingredients and bring to a boil. Reduce the heat and simmer, uncovered, for 2 hours, stirring occasionally. Serves four to six, with leftovers (and it's even better reheated).

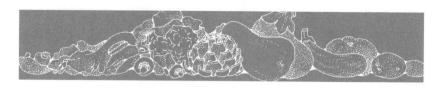

Potato and Leek Soup (and Thou)

...Every man should eat and drink, and enjoy the good of all his labour, it is the gift of God. (Ecclesiastes 3:13)

3 TB unsalted butter

3 cups leeks (white part only), chopped

3 TB flour

5 cups hot water

Salt and pepper to taste

4 cups or more potatoes, peeled and chopped roughly

1 to 2 cups evaporated skimmed milk

Melt butter over medium heat and stir in leeks. Cook slowly for a few minutes without browning the leeks. Add the flour and blend well, again without browning. Gradually add a cup or so of the hot water, blend thoroughly, and add the remaining cups. Stir in the salt and pepper and the potatoes and bring soup to a boil. Simmer partially covered for a good hour, until potatoes are very tender. About a half-hour before serving, add the evaporated skimmed milk for a creamier consistency.

Delicious when accompanied by crusty french bread and a mixed-green salad, this soup serves four with plenty for another repast.

Seize the Day
Split Pea Soup

He that is slow to wrath is of great understanding:
but he that is hasty of spirit exalteth folly. (Proverbs 14:29)

1 pound dried split peas
2 quarts cold water
1 cup chopped carrots
1 cup raw potato, chopped
One medium white onion, chopped
1/2 cup celery, diced
Ham bone, chopped ham or sausage (turkey kielbasa works well)

Rinse and sort peas, then soak for a few minutes. In large soup pot combine drained peas, water, and ham bone (plus ham or sausage). Bring to a boil and simmer covered for 3 hours. Add carrots, potatoes, onion, and celery and continue cooking, uncovered, for another hour. If necessary, thin with additional water or milk.

A hearty pumpernickel or a crusty baguette is all you need to complete this satisfying soup. Serves four, with leftovers enough for another meal.

Thomas Caughey

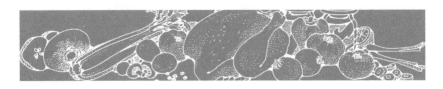

Grandma's Chicken Noodle Soup

For I know the thoughts that I think toward you, saith the Lord, thoughts of peace, and not of evil, to give you an expected end. (Jeremiah 29:11)

Homemade chicken broth

One stewing chicken
One stalk of celery, roughly chopped
Two carrots, roughly chopped
One medium white onion, roughly chopped
Dried parsley, salt, and pepper to taste

Place all above ingredients in large soup pot, cover with cold water, and bring to a boil. Simmer covered for at least an hour. Strain and reserve liquid, discard vegetables, and remove meat from chicken for later use in a casserole or salad. To remove fat

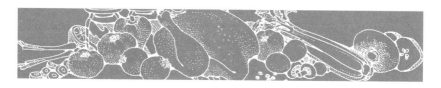

from broth, pour liquid into bowl, cover, and refrigerate overnight. Skim fat off the top and discard.

Chicken Noodle Soup

2 quarts homemade chicken broth
One handful (or more) uncooked extra-fine egg noodles
One lemon
One egg, well beaten

Pour chicken broth into large soup pot and bring to a boil. Reduce to low heat and add egg noodles. Cook for a few minutes until tender. In a separate bowl squeeze juice of lemon and add beaten egg. Gradually incorporate ladlefuls of hot broth into juice mixture until temperature of juice mixture is comparable to broth. Pour juice/broth mixture into broth in soup pot. Continue cooking for at least 10 minutes more. Easily doubled or tripled, this soup will soothe almost any malady, real or imagined.

Joyce Azarian

Crème de la Broccoli Soup

Blessed are the meek: for they shall inherit the earth.
Blessed are they which do hunger and thirst after righteousness:
for they shall be filled. (Matthew 5:5,6)

8 TB unsalted butter or margarine
One large white onion, chopped
Five medium red potatoes, peeled and cubed
4 cups fresh broccoli, cleaned and chopped thinly
4 cups fresh or canned chicken broth
2 cups low-fat milk
Sour cream for garnish

In a large soup pot melt butter over medium-low heat and saute onion and potatoes until soft. Add broccoli and broth and bring to a boil, then simmer until broccoli is tender. Let cool and then puree mixture in a blender or mixer. Return mixture to pot and add milk. Heat through and adjust flavor if necessary, adding more milk or broth. Ladle into soup bowls and top each with a generous dollop of sour cream.

Serves six to eight.

Therese H. Cerbie

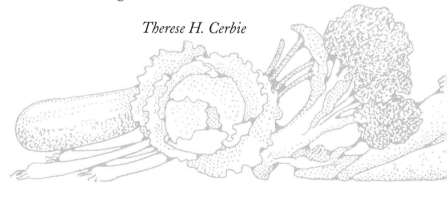

Navy Blazer Bean and Ham Soup

In the world ye shall have tribulation: but be of good cheer;
I have overcome the world. (John 16:33)

1 pound navy beans, rinsed and sorted
1 TB extra-virgin olive oil
Four medium carrots, chopped
Two cloves garlic, minced
One large white onion, chopped
Two medium potatoes, chopped
Italian canned tomatoes, chopped, with juice
1/2 pound cooked ham, chopped
Salt and pepper to taste
1 tsp dried basil
8 to 10 cups cold water

Comfort Food

Place the navy beans in a medium saucepan, add water to cover, and bring to a boil. Turn off heat and let stand, covered, for 30 minutes. Drain water from beans and set aside.

Meanwhile, in a large soup pot, heat the oil over medium heat and add the carrots, onion, garlic, and potatoes. Saute until tender. Add the navy beans, ham, tomatoes and juice (number per your preference), basil, salt and pepper to taste, and the water to cover. Bring to a boil, then reduce heat to a simmer and cook, covered, for approximately 3 hours.

Serves six, with ample leftovers.

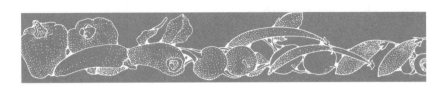

Mellow Mashed Potatoes and Gravy

As far as the east is from the west, so far hath he removed our transgressions from us. (Psalm 103:12)

Five to six medium potatoes, peeled and chopped
Water to cover
Pinch of salt
2 to 3 TB unsalted butter, melted
Skim milk

Gravy

One can chicken or beef broth, slightly chilled
2 TB cornstarch
1/2 cup cold water
Black pepper to taste

Comfort Food

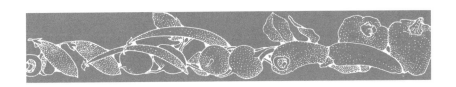

Place potatoes in large saucepan and cover with cold water, adding a pinch of salt. Bring to a boil, then reduce heat to a simmer and cover. Cook until potatoes are extremely tender (a prick of a fork will cause potato to fall apart), approximately 40 minutes. Drain well and return to saucepan, uncovered, and reduce to lowest heat. Allow potatoes to give up more moisture and then mash well with a potato masher, preferably. Add melted butter and then stir in milk, adding more as time passes to achieve desired consistency. Add salt and pepper to taste. Serves four hungry comfort seekers (this is possibly the ultimate comfort food!). For additional soothing, make gravy.

To prepare gravy, first scoop off fat from broth and discard. Pour broth into small saucepan and begin to heat. In a bowl, mix cornstarch in cold water, making sure mixture is free of any lumps. Pour the cornstarch mixture into the broth and add pepper and desired spices as well. Bring to a boil, stirring constantly with a whisk until gravy thickens.

Retro Rice Pilaf

The Lord is the portion of mine inheritance and of my cup: thou maintainest my lot. (Psalm 16:5)

Two fistfuls of extra-fine egg noodles
4 TB unsalted butter (half-stick)
1 1/2 cups long-grained rice (not instant)
Salt and white pepper to taste
3 cups canned or fresh chicken broth and water

In 2-quart saucepan over low heat melt butter and stir in egg noodles until lightly browned. Add rice, salt and pepper, and broth and water. Stir well, cover, and bring to a boil. Lower heat to a simmer and cook for 20 minutes or until liquid is completely absorbed. Do not lift lid until at least 20 minutes have expired. Let pilaf rest for 5 to 10 minutes, and then stir well and serve. Serves four.

Arlene Angione

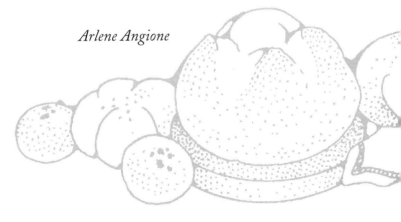

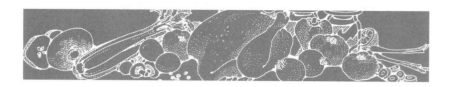

Southern Fried Chicken

For by grace are ye saved through faith;
and that not of yourselves; it is the gift of God; not of works,
lest any man should boast. (Ephesians 2:8,9)

Chicken pieces of your choice, washed and dried
1 to 2 cups flour
1 1/2 tsp salt
1 tsp pepper
1 tsp garlic salt

Comfort Food

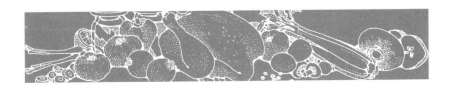

In a brown paper bag combine all ingredients except chicken. Adjust amounts according to the number of pieces you are cooking. Place two to three pieces of chicken into the bag at a time and shake vigorously.

Fry in hot vegetable oil in a heavy iron skillet, if possible. Do not turn chicken frequently. Cook until golden brown on one side, and then turn.

Ellen Nelson

Cabbage of Courage Sandwich

Jesus said unto him, If thou canst believe,
all things are possible to him that believeth. (Mark 9:23)

One-half head of cabbage, shredded
1 1/2 pints heavy cream
1 1/2 TB unsalted butter
One medium white onion, chopped
1 TB caraway seed
Salt and white pepper to taste
Pumpernickel bread, sliced and toasted
Parmesan cheese (optional)

Saute onion and cabbage in butter over medium-low heat. When onion is translucent lower burner to low heat and add cream. Slowly cook until cabbage is soft. Season with caraway seed and salt and pepper.

Spread cabbage mixture on pumpernickel slices; sprinkle a small amount of Parmesan on top if desired. Brown slightly in broiler.

Serves four, but can be easily doubled to accommodate a larger or hungrier crowd.

Cooper Conway

Comfort Food

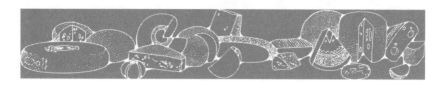

Old-Fashioned Macaroni and Cheese with Tomatoes

How much better is it to get wisdom than gold!
and to get understanding rather to be chosen than silver!
(Proverbs 16:16)

4 cups elbow macaroni
3 TB unsalted butter
3 TB flour
2 1/2 cups low-fat or skim milk
2 cups grated low-fat Cheddar cheese
Ripe tomatoes or canned Italian tomatoes

Cook macaroni according to package instructions, approximately 7 minutes. Drain well.

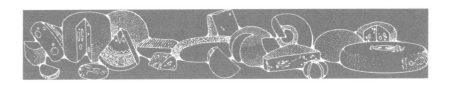

In medium saucepan melt butter over medium-low heat. Stir in flour and cook until bubbly. Remove from heat briefly. Place pan back on burner (increase to medium heat) and add milk gradually, stirring constantly. When mixture has thickened, add grated cheese and stir well until all cheese has melted. Reduce heat to simmer, and season sauce with salt and pepper to taste.

Spray nonstick cooking spray on bottom and sides of 3-quart casserole dish. Place half of drained macaroni in casserole. Add half of the cheese sauce, then combine the remaining macaroni, followed by the remaining sauce. Stir together. Top with chopped tomatoes.

Cover and bake at 375 degrees F for 30 minutes, then uncover and bake until golden brown on top.

Serves four hungry macaroni lovers, with leftovers, or six average appetites.

Cecile Gerdes Johnson

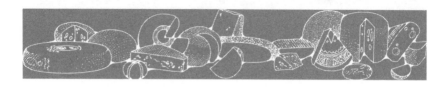

Heartfelt Ham
and Scalloped Potatoes

And having food and raiment let us be therewith content.
(1 Timothy 6:8)

3 TB unsalted butter

One large white onion, chopped

3 TB flour

Salt and pepper to taste

2 cups low-fat or skim milk

2 cups grated low-fat Cheddar cheese

Six medium potatoes, peeled and sliced 1/4 inch thick

2 cups cooked ham, chopped or sliced thin

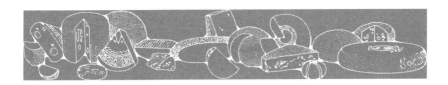

Preheat oven to 375 degrees F.

In a large saucepan over low-medium heat, melt the butter and cook the onion until soft. Be careful not to brown onion. Stir in flour and salt and pepper and mix well. Remove from heat for a minute then return to burner and gradually add milk, stirring constantly until the sauce is smooth. As the sauce begins to thicken, add the cheese and stir well. When cheese has melted and sauce is quite thick, reduce heat to a simmer until you are ready to combine with other ingredients.

Spray a 3-quart casserole dish with nonstick cooking spray. Begin alternating layers of potatoes, ham, and the cheese sauce. Stir layers together slightly. Bake, covered, for 45 minutes. Remove cover and continue baking 25 minutes or so, until the top is a golden brown.

Serves four to six, with usually few if any leftovers.

Pioneer Pot Roast

But thou, O Lord, art a God full of compassion, and gracious, longsuffering, and plenteous in mercy and truth. (Psalm 86:15)

3- to 4-pound beef roast (the best cut available)
One envelope dried onion soup mix
One large white onion, chopped roughly
Three cloves garlic, peeled and chopped
One bay leaf
2 tsp thyme and basil
Black pepper to taste
Beef broth or dry red wine
Water

Preheat oven to 350 degrees F.

Place all of the above ingredients into 3- or 4-quart casserole, covering with equal amounts of beef broth or red wine and cold water. Cover casserole and bake for a good 4 hours. (Take a peek from time to time and add more water if necessary. It's also a good idea to rotate roast in casserole.) Remove roast and place on a heated platter.

Serves plenty, but be sure to plan on leftovers (*see* Beef Stew with Dumplings). Toward that end, pour cooking liquid into clean bowl, cover, and refrigerate.

Beatific Beef Stew (with a Halo of Dumplings)

For whatsoever is born of God overcometh the world: and this is the victory that overcometh the world, even our faith. (1 John 5:4)

Beef stew

Leftover cooked beef from Pot Roast, chopped roughly

Four medium carrots, peeled and chopped

One large white onion, chopped

Four large red potatoes, peeled and chopped (add more if desired)

One bay leaf

Salt and pepper to taste

Cooking liquid from Pot Roast, with fat skimmed off

Beef broth, fresh or canned (combined with cooking liquid,
enough to cover stew ingredients)

Dumplings

1 2/3 cups *Bisquick® Reduced Fat* baking mix
2/3 cup skim milk

Combine stew ingredients, altering vegetable portions if desired, into large soup pot. Beef broth and leftover cooking liquid (plus water, if necessary) should cover all ingredients. Bring to a boil and simmer, covered, for at least 2 hours so flavors are nicely blended.

About a half-hour before serving mix dumpling ingredients until a soft dough forms. Drop by spoonfuls onto boiling stew and reduce heat. Cook uncovered for 10 minutes, and then cover and cook for 10 minutes more.

Chicken "Take Fifty" Tetrazzini

The Lord hath appeared of old unto me, saying,
Yea, I have loved thee with an everlasting love: therefore
with lovingkindness have I drawn thee. (Jeremiah 31:3)

7 ounces (half a package) spaghetti or linguine

1 TB extra-virgin olive oil

1/2 cup white onion, finely chopped

One green pepper, cut into small strips

One red pepper, cut into small strips

3 TB white flour

1 cup skim milk

1 cup evaporated skimmed milk

1/2 tsp salt

1/2 tsp black pepper

2 cups cooked boneless skinless chicken breast, chopped

1 cup frozen peas, defrosted

Grated Parmesan cheese

Comfort Food

Cook the pasta according to package instructions; drain well. Arrange the cooked pasta in a rectangular baking dish.

In a large skillet or saucepan warm the oil and saute the onion and red and green peppers until the vegetables are somewhat softened. Stir in the flour and slowly add the skim milk and evaporated milk. Bring to a boil, stirring constantly, and cook for 5 minutes. Turn off heat and stir in the salt, black pepper, chicken, and peas. Pour this mixture over the pasta and sprinkle liberally with Parmesan cheese. Bake at 300 degrees F for approximately 40 to 45 minutes.

Serves four to six.

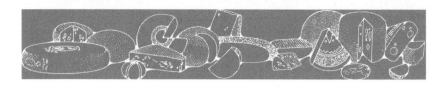

Let's Stay Home Lasagna Roll

In as much as ye have done it unto one of the least of these my brethren, ye have done it unto me.
(Matthew 25:40)

1 pound ground beef
3/4 cup white onion, chopped
One to two cloves garlic, chopped
1/2 tsp basil
1/2 tsp oregano
Salt and pepper to taste
One 6-ounce can tomato paste

Brown meat with onion and garlic and drain off fat. Add other ingredients listed above and simmer uncovered for 5 minutes.

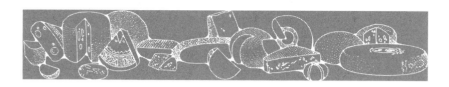

1 cup nonfat cottage cheese
One egg
1/2 cup grated Parmesan cheese

In a separate bowl combine the above ingredients for the cheese filling.

Two cans crescent-style rolls (8 rolls per can)
Four to six slices part-skim Mozzarella cheese

Unroll crescent rolls and piece sections of dough together on ungreased cookie sheet, overlapping edges to form a 15 x 13-inch rectangle. Press edges and perforations to seal. Spread half of meat filling down center of dough, leaving approximately 2 inches on top and bottom. Top with cheese filling, then add remaining meat filling. Place slices of Mozzarella over meat. Fold in edges of rectangle dough and pull long sides of dough over filling, overlapping edges. Pinch dough to seal. Bake at 375 degrees F for 20 to 25 minutes or until golden brown.

Comfort Food

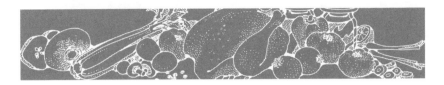

Chicken aah la King

*But ye are a chosen generation, a royal priesthood, an holy nation, a
peculiar people; that ye should shew forth the praises of him who hath
called you out of darkness into his marvellous light. (1 Peter 2:9)*

1/4 cup white onion, chopped
One medium green bell pepper, chopped
3 TB unsalted butter
3 TB flour
2 cups fresh or canned chicken broth
3/4 cup skim milk
2 cups cooked chicken, roughly chopped
2 TB chopped pimento

Comfort Food

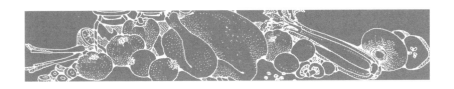

In medium saucepan melt butter and cook onion and green pepper until tender. Blend in flour and cook for a few minutes, stirring constantly. Remove from heat for a minute, then return to medium heat and stir in broth and milk a little at a time. Cook, stirring diligently, until sauce has thickened. Add remaining ingredients and heat through, stirring often.

Pour over toast or egg noodles. Serves four.

Thomas Caughey

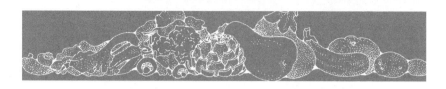

German Potato Salad, Natürlich!

*And seek not ye what ye shall eat, or what ye shall drink,
neither be ye of doubtful mind. But rather seek ye the kingdom of
God; and all these things shall be added unto you.*
(Luke 12:29, 31)

1/2 pound bacon, diced
Five large red potatoes, cooked in their skins
One medium white onion, chopped
Salt and pepper to taste
1 tsp sugar
1/2 cup white vinegar
One egg, well beaten

Comfort Food

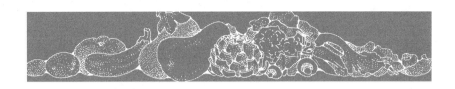

Combine egg, vinegar, sugar, and salt and pepper and set aside. Saute bacon in large saute pan until brown and crispy and drain of fat. Stir in vinegar mixture with bacon. Peel cooked potatoes and dice, then add the chopped onion. Add this mixture to the saute pan contents. Simmer covered for several minutes until heated thoroughly.

This dish becomes complete when accompanied by a mixed-green salad. Serves four.

Cecile Gerdes Johnson

Tuna Cheese Imperial Casserole

For God hath not given us the spirit of fear; but of power,
and of love, and of a sound mind. (2 Timothy 1:7)

8 ounces wide egg noodles

1/2 cup unsalted butter or margarine

5 TB flour

2 1/2 cups low-fat milk

1 tsp salt

1/4 tsp black pepper

8 ounces cream cheese or Neufchâtel (low-fat) cheese

One 14-ounce can of tuna, drained and flaked

2 TB fresh chives, chopped

1/2 cup pimento-stuffed green olives, sliced

6 ounces Muenster cheese, sliced

Four slices white or whole-wheat bread, cubed

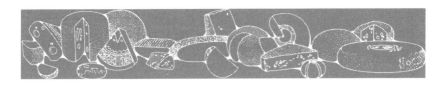

Cook noodles according to package directions; drain well. In medium saucepan, over medium-low heat, melt 5 TB butter or margarine. Gradually add flour, and then milk, stirring constantly, until sauce has thickened. Bring to a boil and let cook for 1 minute. Add salt and pepper.

Slice cream cheese and add to sauce, stirring until melted. Stir in tuna, chives, and olives and remove from heat. Spread 3/4 cup of this mixture across bottom of a buttered baking dish. Layer ingredients as follows: half the noodles, half the remaining sauce, half the Muenster; then the remaining noodles, half the remaining sauce, the rest of the Muenster, and top with the remaining sauce. Melt 3 TB butter or margarine in a medium saute pan and add bread cubes; toss lightly with a fork. Sprinkle buttered cubes over casserole. Bake uncovered at 350 degrees F for 30 minutes or until bubbly. Serves eight.

Lynn Hoehlein

"Braisen" Pork Chops

*Have not I commanded thee? Be strong and of a good courage;
be not afraid, neither be thou dismayed: for the Lord thy God
is with thee whithersoever thou goest. (Joshua 1:9)*

Four to six pork chops, 1 inch thick
1 TB vegetable oil
2 to 3 cups apple cider
One stick of cinnamon
Three cloves
The peel of half an orange
Salt and pepper to taste

Saute chops until nicely browned. Pour apple cider over chops and add cinnamon, cloves, the orange peel, and salt and pepper as well to saute pan. Cook over medium heat until mixture is bubbly. Lower flame to lowest setting and simmer, covered, for 2 to 3 hours.

Serves four.

Cooper Conway

Zucchini the Zealot Low-Fat Bread

I press toward the mark for the prize of the high calling of God in Christ Jesus. (Philippians 3:14)

1/2 cup white sugar
1/2 cup brown sugar
1/2 cup vegetable oil
1/2 cup applesauce

Preheat oven to 375 degrees F. Cream above ingredients together.

Three eggs
1/2 cup skim milk
1 tsp vanilla extract

Add these ingredients and beat well.

Comfort Food

2 1/2 cups flour
1/2 tsp allspice
1/2 tsp salt
2 tsp baking soda
1/2 tsp cinnamon
6 TB cocoa
2 cups zucchini, washed and shredded

Mix together and add to previous mixture. Using nonstick cooking spray, spray two loaf pans. Pour in batter and bake 45 to 60 minutes until toothpick inserted in center comes out clean.

Serves six to eight, and is even more comforting when accompanied by a steaming cup of tea.

Cooper Conway

Rest Assured Rice Pudding

*Every good gift and every perfect gift is from above,
and cometh down from the Father of lights, with whom
is no variableness, neither shadow of turning. (James 1:17)*

1/2 gallon milk
1 3/4 cups white rice
2 cups white sugar
Two eggs
1 TB vanilla extract
2 TB cornstarch
1/4 cup milk (used separately)

Pour 1/2 gallon of milk into large saucepan. Add sugar and rice and bring to a boil. Reduce heat and cook for approximately 45 minutes, stirring occasionally.

In a mixing bowl beat the eggs well and add the vanilla extract. Dilute the cornstarch in 1/4 cup milk in a separate bowl and add to the egg mixture. Slowly pour the egg mixture into the rice mixture, stirring constantly. As pudding begins to thicken, turn off the heat. Pour pudding into a serving dish, sprinkle with cinnamon, and allow to cool.

Dora Kontogiannis

Luscious Lemon Cups

*For ye shall...be led forth with peace: the mountains and the hills
shall break forth before you into singing, and all the trees of the field
shall clap their hands. (Isaiah 55:12)*

1 cup sugar
2 TB unsalted butter
Three eggs, separated
1 1/2 cups low-fat milk
5 TB lemon juice (bottled may be used but fresh tastes better)
Rind of one lemon, diced
4 TB flour
Pinch of salt

Preheat oven to 350 degrees F.

In a mixing bowl combine butter, sugar, flour, salt, lemon juice, and rind. Stir in beaten egg yolks mixed with milk. Fold in stiffly beaten egg whites.

Pour mixture into custard cups and then place cups in a pan of lukewarm water. Bake approximately 35 minutes, or until top is nicely browned.

To serve, invert cups on dessert plates and perhaps garnish with a sprig of mint. Serves four.

Karen Sokol

Tart Cherry Pie (with Buttery Pie Crust)

*But as many as received him, to them gave he power
to become the sons of God, even to them
that believe on his name. (John 1:12)*

Pie Crust

4 cups flour
Two sticks unsalted butter or margarine
3/4 cup shortening
One egg
1 TB white vinegar
1/2 cup cold water

Mix ingredients together. Form into four equal-sized balls.
Freeze for later use or refrigerate for a half-hour before rolling
out. Roll out thinly on well-floured waxed paper. Use waxed
paper to aid in transfer to 9-inch aluminum pie pan.

Comfort Food

Pie Filling

Two 9-inch unbaked pastry crusts (top and bottom)
Two 1-pound cans tart pitted cherries, packed in water
3/4 cup sugar
3 TB cornstarch
1 TB unsalted butter or margarine

Drain cherries, reserving 1 cup of the liquid. Mix sugar, cornstarch, and liquid in medium saucepan. Cook and stir over medium heat until mixture thickens. Stir in butter or margarine and then cherries. Pour into bottom crust, then cover with top crust. Cut air vents in top crust. Cover perimeter with three strips of aluminum foil. Bake at 425 degrees F for 40 minutes. Serves eight.

Thomas Caughey

Chocolate Contentment Bread Pudding

I am come a light into the world, that whosoever believeth on me should not abide in darkness. (John 12:46)

4 cups stale french bread, torn into small pieces
4 cups low-fat milk
1 cup sugar
Four 1-ounce squares unsweetened chocolate, melted
Four eggs
1 tsp vanilla extract
(Optional: 1 TB dark rum)

Soak bread pieces in milk. Meanwhile beat eggs, vanilla extract, and sugar, and then add melted chocolate. Mix well. Combine bread and milk mixture (do not drain milk) and rum (optional) into chocolate mixture and pour into buttered baking dish. Place dish in larger pan and pour boiling water into pan until depth measures approximately 2 inches. Bake at 350 degrees F for 45 minutes or until set.

Serves eight to ten, and don't forget to offer a heaping bowl of homemade whipped cream (to heap on top!).

Peter's Pie

Rejoice evermore. Pray without ceasing. In every thing give thanks: for this is the will of God in Christ Jesus concerning you. (1 Thessalonians 5:16-18)

2/3 cup sugar
2 TB flour
3 TB cornstarch
1/4 tsp salt
2 cups milk
Three egg yolks, beaten
1/2 cup creamy peanut butter
1/2 tsp vanilla extract
1/2 cup real semisweet chocolate chips
One premade 8-inch pie shell, baked

Mix together sugar, flour, cornstarch, and salt until well blended and pour in heavy saucepan. Over medium heat slowly add milk to dry ingredients, stirring constantly. When mixture is bubbly and thickened, add one-quarter of mixture to egg yolks and pour yolk mixture back into greater mixture. Again, stir constantly until mixture is thickened.

Remove from heat and add peanut butter and vanilla extract. Stir until peanut butter has melted. Pour mixture into pie shell, add chocolate chips, and let stand 2 minutes. Swirl chips with a knife to distribute evenly throughout the pie. Cool pie in refrigerator.

Serves eight.

Cooper Conway

Elegant Peach Delight

And now abideth faith, hope, charity, these three;
but the greatest of these is charity. (1 Corinthians 13:13)

One box yellow cake mix
1 1/2 to 1 3/4 sticks margarine, softened
One large can peaches, drained
1 pint sour cream
Three egg yolks
Cinnamon

Combine cake mix and margarine. Press in lightly greased 9- x
12-inch pan. Arrange peaches on top. Beat sour cream and egg
yolks together. Pour over peaches, spreading to sides of the pan.
Sprinkle cinnamon evenly on top. Bake at 350 degrees F for 20
to 30 minutes.

Grace Alford

Comfort Food